# Acknowledgements

 W9-BIX-693

We wish to thank Ben Conn for his vision and support for this project that was drawn up on a napkin over coffee. But his vision was so clearly articulated that developing the project was an easy task for us. Our professional beliefs and his vision collided that morning and we were off on a mission. You now have in your hands the results. So to this end, we dedicate this project to our friend, Ben Conn.

We also want to thank the teachers at Francis Nungester Elementary School in Decatur, AL and Chets Creek Elementary School in Jacksonville, FL for inviting us to witness their classroom libraries in action with our cameras in hand. When children become absorbed in story, they take no notice of adults standing around snapping pictures.

We hope you will find the book helpful as you work to create for your students the best educational journey possible. We truly believe that one of the first tools needed after your dedication and devotion to the teaching profession is the Classroom Library!

Good luck and best wishes!

Lester and Reba

Copyright © 2012 by Lester Laminack and Reba Wadsworth

Cover design by the HF Group
Book design by the HF Group

All rights reserved.

No part of this book may be reproduced in any form or by any electronic or mechanical means including information storage and retrieval systems, without permission in writing from the author. The only exception is by a reviewer, who may quote short excerpts in a review.

Printed in the United States of America

First Printing: August 2012

ISBN-13 978-14569-04609

# Table of Contents

Classroom Libraries

## A Library in the Classroom

Just mention the word library and some people will hear "Shhhhhh!" rushing from the mouth of an unseen adult. "Library" may evoke memories of tall stacks filled with books, a maze of pages and covers and spines. Or perhaps the word, library, evokes that particular musty smell, or the shadowed aisles, a silent tomb for books. Then there's the stereotype of a librarian, glasses attached to a chain perched on the tip of her nose, hair pulled back into a tight bun watching over the books like a guard at Fort Knox.

Or perhaps "library" floods you with memories of a haven, a paradise of pages, a storehouse of stories, a bank vault of books, and all of it just for you. Perhaps "library" evokes memories of adventure, a treasure hunt, hours of time that passed like seconds. For you, the library was not a maze of shadowed aisles, but a territory you navigated with the ease of a long time resident.

Either way, chances are that "library" doesn't evoke memories of a space in the classroom of your childhood. Most of us did not have a classroom library, a space in the room with a collection tailored to the interests and abilities of students.

That has changed and classroom libraries have become an essential component of daily life in school. A classroom library can become a most treasured respite for your students. It can become the "go-to" spot for information, recreation, escape and exploration. We have written this handbook to help you create that kind of space, a classroom library that will make your teaching more effective and more efficient.

With that goal in mind, the classroom library must be attractive, well organized and accessible. It needs to be filled with resources that capture the interests and fit the abilities of your students. It should be the place where children gravitate when there is an open moment in their schedule. An open and inviting space where students are seeking the next treasure to answer a burning question, or searching for the next book in a favorite series, or looking for "that" book—the one you read aloud last Tuesday. The classroom library should be the place where you see children pulling a friend aside and saying, "you've got to read this."

**So what if I do all this work, will it make any difference?**

For those who need "proof" there is general agreement in the professional literature that the classroom library is a key component in the development of reading and writing and, more importantly, in fostering the love of reading. Routman (2003) contends that a classroom library must receive top priority if you expect to have students who become thriving and engaged readers.

The classroom library creates an accessible and familiar space where books are readily available. Familiarity and accessibility naturally increases the amount of time children spend with books and there is ample research supporting the notion that the more time children spend reading, the better readers they become (Neuman, 1999; Routman, 2003).

**Time with books:**

- develops book handling knowledge
- fosters familiarity
- fosters awareness of genre
- fosters awareness of format and structure
- fosters awareness of options and helps establish preferences
- builds confidence
- builds strong readers and strong readers become strong writers

A classroom library enables you to put the best resource in a student's hand on the spot. When students have access at the point of need they are more likely time spend time with books. And research is clear; time spent reading is a key component in the overall development of positive attitudes about reading, increased reading achievement and improved comprehension. In short, access to texts and increased time spent reading are essential to reading success (Cunningham & Stanovich, 1998; Routman, 2003).

Need more proof?  OK, check out these findings (Neuman, 1999). When books are in close proximity to classroom activity:

- time spent reading increased by 60%
- literacy-related activities more than doubled
- letter knowledge, phonemic awareness, concepts of print and writing, and narrative competence increased by 20%.

So let's agree that an accessible classroom library has a dramatic effect on literacy development.

**Quality, variety, accessibility are indispensable**

Time with books is essential, but does it matter which books?  Will anything with pages, a spine and a cover suffice?  NOT!  The collection must be filled with quality texts, writing that is engaging and interesting, and materials that are visually appealing. The most significant growth occurs when students increase both volume of reading (the number of books read) and their reading stamina (the amount of time spent reading) (Allington, 2000).  Therefore, the collection must be something students will be drawn to and it must be sufficient to sustain their interest.

Knowing that we need students to increase both volume and stamina calls for a collection of texts that represents a good variety of formats, topics, genres, and authors.  In addition, if the classroom library is going to become the "go-to" spot, then the collection must include material students can read accurately and fluently.  This, of course, suggests the need for having many of the books in your collection leveled. Access to books that have you can read increases fluency, which is linked to successful comprehension (Allington, 2000).

## Time to talk about what they read

Having an attractive and accessible classroom library invites students to handle the books. Having a sufficient and varied collection will engage their interests and pull them in over and over. The habit of visiting the classroom library boosts the time spent with books, which of course, is necessary to increase reading volume and stamina. When reading volume and stamina increase students are going to be spilling over with enthusiasm for what they have read. And that will result in the need for time devoted to talking about and writing in response to what they have read. When students are given opportunities to talk about what they have read there is even greater gain in overall reading development (Neuman, 1999).

The opportunity to talk about what they have read:

- enhances motivation to read
- provides other perspectives on the text
- scaffolds understanding
- helps the reader clarify thinking about the text
- expands vocabulary
- provides opportunity for civil dialog
- results in a more robust understanding of the text

## Get the picture?

Are you getting the picture here? A well-stocked, accessible classroom library is of primary importance in every classroom. So as you begin to design your classroom give careful consideration to the location and organization of the classroom library. The location needs to be highly accessible and the collection should be organized in a way that makes sense to the students. Remember, the purpose is to make books accessible to your students. And as you are developing the schedule remember that students need both ample time to read and planned opportunities to engage in conversations about what they are reading. After all, why go to the trouble of establishing this amazing resource if you are not going to take advantage of the benefits?

If you are feeling a bit overwhelmed by the idea of collecting the books, getting them organized, creating the space and managing the use of the library, then you may find comfort in the words of Lucy Calkins:

"[T]he most creative environments in our society are not the kaleidoscopic environments in which everything is always changing and complex. They are instead, the predictable and consistent ones - the scholar's library, the researcher's laboratory, the artist's studio. Each of these environments is deliberately kept predictable and simple because the work at hand and the changing interactions around that work are so unpredictable and complex" (1986).

Though she is talking about the structures and routines that form the architecture of the reading/writing workshop, the same can be said of the classroom library [or any work space in the classroom]. The work of learning can be unpredictable and complex, so establishing the classroom library as a simple, consistent and predictable work environment brings stability and comfort to the process. Remember you are creating a resource hub to make life and learning more efficient and effective for students. Success hinges on the ease of use and accessibility established through the work you do on the front end.

## OK, Let's Get This Library Started

So now you are ready to get started, but you aren't sure what to do first.  Let's begin thinking about the collection of books/texts the classroom library should offer.  Take a moment and think about one of those famous ice cream shops and all those flavors and the various combinations you can select to create the decadent demise of your diet.  All those flavors are not there because each customer is going to select one scoop of each.  It is unlikely that a customer is going have a scoop of a new flavor each day until all the flavors have been sampled.  It is even more unlikely that a customer will come in time and again until all the possible combinations have been exhausted.  So why have all those flavors and all those combinations?  You create options so that customers have the opportunity to sample, to try new things and branch out.  All those options give customers a reason to return.  After all, it is through the process of sampling that we find our favorites.  Going with friends to the ice cream shop opens new options as they find their favorites as well.  Have you ever been to an ice cream shop with a friend who insists you have to try a flavor she has just discovered?  Sometimes you discover a new favorite.  At other times you have an option you can take off your list.  Options spark exploration.  Exploration opens doors to potentials untapped.

**What's on your menu?**

The same is true for the collection of books/texts in a classroom library. As you gather books include a variety of:

- genres –non-fiction, fiction, poetry, periodicals
- subjects—science, social studies, mathematics, music
- themes—friendship, cycles, conflict, change, conservation
- topics—dogs, dinosaurs, machines, rivers, volcanoes, tornadoes
- formats—poem, feature article, song, script, narrative, recipe, interview, ABC books,
- authors—Gail Gibbons, Eric Carle, Patricia MacLachlan, Kate DiCamillo, Ezra Jack Keats
- illustrators—Ted Lewin, Jon J. Muth, Henry Cole, Denise Fleming, Thomas Locker

In the same way the manager of an ice cream shop will think about the varied tastes of potential customers, we must think about the varied interests and passions of readers who will live among these books and use them daily. We must recognize that we are not selecting on the basis of what WE love. Instead we make selections on the basis of what THEY will use and find engaging. We include new options for them to explore, discover and fall in love with. We gather not with our favorites in mind, but with the notion of helping them discover their favorites. We gather not only with our units in mind, but with the topics they are likely to be passionate about and with the parameters of the standards and curriculum in mind.

## Begin with a check of the inventory

Let's begin with the books that are in your classroom already. Knowing what you have will help you determine where you have gaps to fill. First, bring all the books to the carpet or table and put them in one large pile. Don't worry about the labels on the existing bins or the way they were clustered, just put them in one big pile. We will talk about sorting the books, creating categories/labels and organizing the classroom library in another section. Let's do this one step at a time.

Now take the time to become familiar (or to reacquaint yourself) with the existing books. There may be books you will need to set aside and read before making a decision. And some books may be outdated or worn; these need to be removed from the collection. As you explore the books sort them into four broad categories: non-fiction, fiction, poetry, and periodicals. At this point you will get a general notion of where your resources are.

If you have a healthy number of books in the non-fiction and fiction stacks try sorting each of these stacks into smaller, more specific stacks. As you sort you may find it helpful to consider these headings:

- non-fiction—information, how-to, all about, reference, memoir, biography, autobiography, interviews, essays, feature articles, etc.
- fiction—realistic fiction, historical fiction, adventure, short stories, plays, fables, legends, fairy tales, fantasy, etc.
- poetry—anthologies, edited collections, poet collections, various forms
- favorite series
- thematic—interests, state/district curriculum, standards expectations

## Knowing what you need

As you determine which areas of your collection need to be updated or developed you are ready to begin the process of acquiring new material for the classroom library. We know of no magic formula for selecting books and texts to create the perfect balance in each category. The goal is to create a collection that will support the interests and efforts of your students as they read independently, work on curriculum projects and explore personal interests.

As you begin the process you will need to think about the broad categories and the more specific sections within each category as well.

## Non-fiction

When given choice in reading many students will gravitate toward non-fiction to quench their thirst for finding out about the world around them, understanding how things work and acquiring new information. It is this inquisitive spirit, this sense of unbridled wonder that will fuel the desire to explore and read. Therefore, be conscious of the need to include a healthy portion of non-fiction as you select. If you want to be certain you have ample resources for subject study use your state curriculum/course of study and/or the standards to identify topics. To expand that list use a reading or interest inventory at the beginning of the year to find out what your students are passionate about.

Non-fiction has become increasingly more important in reading instruction, independent reading and subject matter teaching. To round out the non-fiction section of the library search for a balance of topics, subjects and formats in non-fiction to include the following: how-to, all about, information, reference, memoir, biography, autobiography, interviews, essays, feature articles.

## Fiction

We tend to think of fiction as "story" and writing that is "not true." While this is accurate it isn't complete. Fiction is a broad heading that includes realistic fiction, historical fiction, adventure stories, short stories, mysteries, plays, fables, fairy tales, folk tales, and the like. So it is likely that many existing classroom libraries will have more fiction than any other category. As you acquire new texts and add to your library be aware of the various types of fiction you can make available.

Think like the manager of that ice cream shop we mentioned and push beyond the expected vanilla and chocolate. Offer new possibilities and create new options for your readers. If "story" is all you have you may find the history buff doesn't read much in your class and the adventure junky doesn't visit the classroom library.

## Poetry

No classroom library would be complete without a generous portion of poetry. Poetry should be part of everyday routines in the classroom; not shelved away on reserve waiting for the poetry unit in writing workshop or brought out only in April for national poetry month. We find that the poetry collection is often a neglected section in classroom libraries.

As you layer poetry into your classroom library remember to include books of poetry by a single poet, anthologies, and edited collections organized by topic or theme or form. Remember to consider all areas of the curriculum and to include several poets.

Of course we recommend having a large collection of poetry books to support young writers in the writing workshop, but we also encourage featuring one poem each week throughout the year. A featured poem visited each day provides the opportunity for layers of work around the forms and qualities of poetry, language play, word choice, specificity and image rich vocabulary. For more details on how to make this a daily practice see *Learning Under the Influence of Language and Literature*, Laminack and Wadsworth (2006); *Climb Inside a Poem,* Heard and Laminack (2007).

**Magazines and periodicals**

Magazines and other periodicals are an enticing addition to the classroom collection. Materials that feel more "grown up" and less "school like" make for an appealing and engaging format. In addition, magazines and periodicals provide a contrast to the more familiar or typical structure of books. They offer outstanding illustrations/photographs and provide ample opportunity for learning about text structures and text features. Magazines also offer a less intimidating access to information since the text is typically shorter and frequently interspersed with charts, photos, captions and diagrams.

As a teacher you will find that periodicals make an excellent and efficient resource because, in addition to the content, many periodicals offer an array of genre options within a single source. For example, you often find poems, feature articles, activities, procedural text, fiction, and comments from readers in a single issue. Including magazines and periodicals in the classroom library is a plus any time. But when resources are limited, you have engaging material that provides an introduction to the topic/theme in a structure that offers support for a range of readers and interests.

Some of the most well- known magazines for children include:

- *Zoo Books*
- *National Geographic for Kids*
- *Time for Kids*
- *Sports Illustrated for Kids*
- *Ranger Rick* (ages 7-14)
- *My Big Back Yard* (ages 4-7)
- *Animal Baby* (pre-k/k)
- *Cobblestone*
- *Cricket*
- *Spider*
- *Zoobies* (preschool)
- *Zootles* (kindergarten)
- *Zoobooks* (elementary)
- *Weekly Readers* (available for every grade level)

**Mix and match a few flavors (text sets and thematic collections)**

Think outside the bins (pun intended). As you begin growing your collection take a look at the interests of your students and the themes that seem to work across areas of the curriculum. Think about pulling books from their "home" bin and placing them together in sets for a period of time.

Consider a few text sets or thematic sets in your collection. A set of books (3-5 titles) selected to explore a topic in some depth offering various perspectives can make learning more robust. A set may be assembled to invite students to explore a topic or theme through multiple perspectives. In addition, students have the opportunity to explore various formats, text features, structures, and writing styles. This, of course, scaffolds the opportunity for comparing and contrasting information, for categorizing and classifying information, and for summarizing and synthesizing information.

A text set can help you meet both the curricular expectations and the interests of students. For example, you may assemble a text set on pumpkins and another on bats. Both topics are likely to emerge as an interest in the fall. If the curriculum does not include a study of pumpkins, but does require a study of the life cycle of plants the set will satisfy both the interests of students and the expectations of the curriculum. Likewise, the specific topic "bats" may not appear in the curriculum whereas a study of mammals or animals or habits or nocturnal animals is more likely. The bats text set allows for exploration in any of these while engaging students in a topic of interest.

Clearly these text sets can be used for specific teaching points; however, it is sufficient to have them available for children to select during free reading time. Text sets can be organized into bins by theme or topic and be used to open areas of interest that will eventually find itself into the reading, research and writing of your students.

When the class or a group is in the midst of a specific study you might consider putting out supplementary books and other texts on the content being studied. Think like a marketing executive and capture the students while interest in the topic is high. For instance, if you are studying insects, bring in books about insects from the school or local library. Include literary fiction and poetry and magazine selections that relate to the topic. You could read *Water Dance* or *Cloud Dance* by Thomas Locker, for example, during a unit on weather. Always be on the lookout for texts that fit into your core curriculum as you add to your classroom library.

For more information on using text sets or thematic collections see *Reading Aloud Across the Curriculum,* Laminack and Wadsworth, (2006); *Unwrapping the Read Aloud*, Laminack (2007).

## Acquiring Books

We have heard Richard Allington say each classroom library should have approximately **1,500** books. We will pause here for a moment and let you catch your breath. (PAUSE—breathe in, breathe out). Others in the field have been quoted as saying a classroom library would be sufficient with 20 books per child. But we love children's literature and we have seen the power of a rich and robust classroom library, so we agree with Allington. If you are going to err in this situation it is wiser to err on the high side, in favor of the students who will benefit. When literature is thoughtfully and intentionally selected to create a rich, robust and balanced classroom library, reading will become the window to the world. And that window will open vistas that cannot be experienced through contrived, scripted programs, basal programs and survey textbooks for the subject areas.

### Keep the focus on quality and take it one step at a time

OK, we heard that whoosh of air escaping as you read that first sentence. We heard that exasperated whisper, "1500 books! Where the heck will I get 1500 books? Are these guys crazy?" Pause. Now breathe and don't panic. Even if you are just beginning in a new classroom and you have absolutely no books to begin a new school year, remember Rome wasn't built in a day and neither will your classroom library! So start where you are. Do what you can as you can manage, but keep your focus on the quality of what you include and remember to select with balance in mind. It is far better to select quality books from outstanding authors slowly than to stock your classroom with bargain books that do not meet the needs and interests of your students nor the expectations of the curriculum.

**Where to find what you need**

When you are ready to begin selecting books, first check with your principal and ask if funds are available. Even if you think they won't be, ask any way, you never know. And remember no one knows your needs if you don't voice them. It is a good idea to be on record with what you need to support the learning lives of your students. Perhaps follow up the conversation with an email to confirm what was said and thanking her or him for considering your request. You may even ask your principal to keep you on the wish list in the event funds should be made available in the future. Also ask in the email if your principal knows of other sources you could tap.

**Let the search begin**

Once you know the facts you can begin to get creative. Here are some tips that have worked for other teachers when establishing a new library or extending an existing collection:

- Map out the types of books or the specific titles you will need to support the curriculum and check out the site for the company offering this handbook on developing classroom libraries. You can find their site at www.classroomlibrarycompany.com. You can find most of the materials in this book on sale. Books, Bins, Labels and Templates.

- Check the **want ads** each day for **moving sales**. Books are heavy and expensive to move so you may get lucky and find a great deal. It is possible to find a treasure trove of quality children's books. Invest a few Saturday mornings and hit a few moving sales and yard/garage sales. You may be pleasantly surprised by how often you will come away with a treasure.

- Go to **Goodwill**, the **Salvation Army** store and other thrift shops and check for children's books. If you find a source in one of these go back often, make friends with the clerk and ask to be notified when new ones come in.

- Check out **discount stores**. We have found that TJ Maxx, Tuesday Morning, and Kohl's have a good children's section and we have been known to find great books at good prices
- Check **eBay** for books on the topics you are seeking.

- Check **Book Closeout**, another source somewhat similar to eBay, for discounted titles. Go to www.bookcloseout.com and type in the title or the author's name. You will be prompted if the books you are searching for are available. And for the record, Reba has found many treasures on this site. These two resources (eBay and Book Closeout) are helpful to fill-in with desired books, but not a great source for developing the core of your library. Books from each of these sources are inexpensive; even with shipping you will save money. The same is true for used books on Amazon. However, be careful to check the shipping fees to be sure you are getting the best deal.

- **Scholastic** offers a **book club magazine** each month. The selection of titles varies from month to month and the cost of books is very reasonable. Each child takes home a sheet listing the titles/cost of the books for that month. The more students order, the more points you are given. The points can be redeemed for books. Scholastic also sporadically offers a package of 100 books for $99.00. There will be one package for each grade level. You are not able to select titles for the package so you can never be certain which titles will arrive. While this is a good way to begin building volume it is not an effective method for building the core of your library.

- Another source is to let **parents** know that you appreciate books as gifts or as donations to the classroom. Suggest they put a book in honor of their child in the classroom library. Design a bookplate especially for this purpose and make a big deal of it. Always have a **list of desired books** for everyone to choose from when making a donation. We've seen teachers who put a big apple outside their classroom door at Open House with a **wish list**. In addition to extra paper or other school supplies, suggest several books (new or used) you would like to have for the classroom this year. You may also post a wish list on the classroom web site. Make note on that list when a title is donated and use the opportunity to model civility by having the class send a thank you note to the donor.

- Your **local public library** usually culls the collection and has an annual sale. In these events you can pick up books at an unbelievable price. Libraries withdraw books for various reasons and many are still in good condition.

- Ask your **school librarian** for help. She/he may have some withdrawn books that you can have. If that is not the case, ask if you can check out a large number of books that you will gladly rotate back to the library every few weeks. Remember books are meant to be in the hands of the children and not stored on a shelf.

- And **used bookstores** often have a section devoted to children's literature.

# Planning the Physical Space for Your Classroom Library

Yikes! What a mess.  A scene like this one greets teachers all over the country each year as the school year begins.  Though it may look daunting the situation actually presents an opportunity to envision the environment you want to establish for your children. Clearly it will take creativity, physical effort and resources but "…when we create classroom environments that are attractive, comfortable, and purposeful, we will surely reap the results of our efforts" (Taberski, 2000).

## Picture it

We have a challenge for you. Before you begin setting up the physical space make a photo of each piece of furniture and all the materials you plan to have out and available to children.  Print them out, take them with you and leave the building.  Go someplace and have a beverage.  Sit and sip and sort them into three stacks.

- First stack-- place only those images of furniture and materials you deem *absolutely essential* to the success of your students.
- Second stack--place those images of the items you consider *very important, but not essential*.  This stack may contain images of materials that will be essential to a particular study or time of year.
- Third stack--place *everything else*. Even if you are not a new teacher and this is your classroom from last year, consider purging old and damaged stuff. We both know from experience that old

stuff becomes useless clutter without you even realizing it. Don't keep old furniture that is broken or scarred badly unless a new coat of paint will make it attractive, and even then, keep it only if it is useful. Think about how things are used and how often. Think about how you could consolidate uses for some furniture and reduce the number of desks, chairs, tables, storage cabinets, and file drawers using up valuable space.

Now return to the first stack and place these images in priority order. What are your *most important "essentials"*? If one *had* to go, what could you weed out? Have you included the storage and display space for your classroom library? Will that work in existing shelving/display or does it require that you acquire some?

## Work it

It's time to take action. Return to the room and remove everything in the third stack. Set those things in the hallway and invite others to take them or ask that they be placed in storage. Just get them out of the room. Now remove everything in the second stack. Place those items in the hallway. Put a "do not remove" sign on them if necessary. All that remains should be the most essential items.

Pause for a moment.  Use masking tape or the blue painters tape and section off the areas.  Think about how each are will be used, how many students will be there at one time and which furniture/materials are most useful to the function you envision.  Now place your "most essential" items.  Once they are placed pause again and consider the room with all your students added.  What is not present that will enhance the usefulness of a given area? Now bring in the items from the second stack—*as needed*.

Through this process you may decide to move items from the second stack into the third one.  Think back to the quote from Lucy Calkins (1986)…"the most creative environments in our society are not the kaleidoscopic environments in which everything is always changing and complex. They are instead, the predictable and consistent ones…"  This is one situation where more is not always better.  In fact, more furniture and more material may contribute to more clutter and more distraction, which may be counterproductive.

As you continue layering in furniture, equipment and other materials remember, the classroom library area must be very purposefully arranged and organized around the idea of providing a balanced literacy learning opportunity for your students.  We've heard teachers across the country comment that there is not enough space for a classroom library.  Perhaps you've already heard a little voice saying that in the back of your mind.  We remind you, space is a premium and it should be used wisely with maximum benefit for children.  And most of us know that we find time, resources, and space for those things that become a priority in our lives.

**A few things to keep in mind:**

- Visualize traffic flow
- Cluster individual desks or place tables to maximize floor space and tap the potential of collaborative learning
- Consider creating multiuse areas with the shelving for the classroom library
- Identify a couple of places in the room where several shelves could be arranged to create a reading area, a conference space, an area for small group work, etc. without becoming an obstacle to the flow of classroom traffic
- Consider having the library as the backdrop for a meeting area large enough for the class to gather for mini-lessons, read aloud experiences and class meetings

Regardless of how you decide to set it up, the area should send a message that reading is valued in this classroom and serve as a visual reminder of your core beliefs as a teacher.

## Organize it

When you have selected the area it's time to begin thinking about how to organize that space so that it draws students in. Here are a few things to consider:

- Your spot--this may be a large beanbag, director's chair, club chair or rocker where you can sit to lead mini-lessons, hold class meetings and present read-aloud experiences. Think of sitting there every day and select something you will be comfortable in. Think also of space. If you find your chair is the biggest thing in the space you should consider other options.

- Beanbags for students--you don't need one for every student. You and your students can develop a system to determine who gets to sit on them and when.

- Lamps—the soft glow of lamps in a room creates a coziness that is inviting. One or two lamps in the classroom library area should be ample. Position them so there is ample lighting for selecting books, reading, or working on projects.

- Throw pillows—pillows add a touch of comfort, color, and texture to the area. In addition, pillows can create boundaries of personal space when used to sit on. They also make the space cozy for reading and project work.
- Book bins—plastic bins that sit on shelves to hold the books. We prefer colorless transparent bins that allow you to see into the bin and reveal the contents. From a distance you will notice books, not bins and, after all, books are what a library is about. The end of the bin facing out will be labeled to indicate the author, category, topic, theme or genre.
- Shelves—selecting adequate shelving is important. If possible, choose shelves that are no more than shoulder high on your students and no more than waist high on you. This size is crucial for two important reasons. First, you are developing a space that fosters independence, so the space itself should be accessible to students without adult assistance. Second, you need to be able to scan the room and have a clear view of every area when standing. If the shelves are in good shape and the finish is in good condition you are ready to begin. However, you may need/want to paint the shelving to make it more attractive.
- If you design the space as a multiuse area, then you will also need room for an easel for anchor charts and the Morning Message.

Invest the time to plan this area. It should become the heart of your classroom, a hub of activity where students with gather throughout the day for reading, to gather resources, for project work and again for each of your whole class meetings.

For additional ideas go on the Internet, search *classroom libraries* and click on images. The photos offer several options for configuration, color scheme, organization and presentation. A visit to these virtual classroom libraries will help you decide what will work best for you. So before you paint the first shelf, purchase the first basket or make the first label you will have a plan and avoid costly mistakes.

While you are on the web searching for ideas, notice how the books are displayed. Most of the books are facing out like products in the grocery store. Not spine out like books shelved in the main school or public library. Notice the displays of books in your local bookstore. New and featured titles are displayed face out. Most readers, of any age, will go to the 'face out' books first. Remember, you are trying to invite students in, to hook them on books, to draw their attention to the collection, so think advertising. This one works magic. Why do you think cereal is sitting on the shelf 'face out'? Could it be they want to appeal to the buyer? Of course, it is! Try this yourself. Go to your local bookstore and walk into the children's section, notice which books capture your attention first. We bet you will go right to the ones facing out, the ones begging for your attention. Children are no different.

As you design your library consider using the shelves as borders to define the area. Think about how the space within and around the library will be used before placing the shelving. And remember to create a configuration that will enable you to see all students regardless of where you are working in the room.

## Sorting Books for the Classroom Library

Now you've created the space, acquired the books and you are faced with the task of deciding how to sort them into categories that will make the most sense for your students. Does it help to know that each year many teachers sort and rearrange their collections trying to find the best system to maximize accessibility? You will discover one system works for one teacher and one group of students yet may not work for you or your class. And the system that works this year with this group may not be the most effective with another group in another year. So explore several options before deciding how to organize. Remember the idea here is to create a system that will maximize accessibility and circulation. A beautiful display of unused books is no more beneficial than empty shelves.

When it comes to sorting your books, there is no one right way or best way. The point is to create a system that enables you and your students to know what you have and where it is. Ease of use is the goal.

Together we have over sixty years of experience in education (Wow, that makes us sound old). So we are drawing from years of experience in our own classrooms and the classrooms of teachers across the county as we offer these recommendations for sorting your books.

Think back to the sort we suggested for your existing books to determine what you have and where your collection is lacking. In that sort you began with four large stacks (non-fiction, fiction, poetry, magazine/periodicals) and then, if there was a sufficient quantity, divided each of those stacks into subsets:

- **non-fiction**—information, how-to, all about, reference, memoir, biography, autobiography, interviews, essays, feature articles, etc.
- **fiction**—realistic fiction, historical fiction, adventure, short stories, plays, fables, legends, fairy tales, fantasy, etc.
- **poetry**—anthologies, edited collections, poet collections, various forms
- **favorite series**
- **thematic**—interests, state/district curriculum, standards expectations

Now you are ready to merge your existing books with newly acquired ones and organize the collection. Begin with those existing stacks and sort them into bins by categories. As you create the spaces on your shelves designate sections for:

- Bins of non-fiction books (include any form of non-fiction unless there is sufficient interest and quantity to create a specific subset of non-fiction such as how-to books, all about/information books, etc.)
- Bins of biographies/autobiographies/memoirs (a typical subset of your non-fiction)
- Bins of fiction books (include any form of fiction unless there is sufficient interest and quantity to create a specific category of fiction such as historical fiction or adventure stories, etc.)
- Bins of fairy tales, folk tales, legends, myths (a typical subset of your fiction)
- Bins of series books
- Bins of poetry books
- Bins of song books (especially for young children)
- Bins of author study collections (which may be a subset pulled from several bins)
- Bins of thematic/topic collections (ex. friendship, cycles, conflict, change, conservation/ dogs, dinosaurs, machines, rivers, volcanoes, tornadoes, etc. which may be a subset of several bins)
- Bins of leveled books (we will offer suggestions for leveling literature)

Now that you have the books sorted it is time to label the bins so children can find what they are looking for.

## Label it

All the books in your classroom library are now neatly housed in a bin with the cover facing out and readily available to every student.  The next step is to create a labeling system that that makes sense to your students. Keep the grade level and developmental needs of your class in mind as you design the labels and the scheme for organizing the bins.

Write the name of each bin on a small white index card with a permanent marker.  Print in clear block letters for ease of reading.  Now place the card on a piece of tag board you have cut as a backing.

One system we've seen used successfully placed an adhesive colored dot on the cover of each book and a matching dot on the label of the bin where the book belongs.  We recommend placing the colored dot in a consistent spot on each book (e.g. upper left corner of the cover or upper right corner of the back).  Some teachers prefer placing the dots on the back to keep the cover completely visible; this, of course, is a matter of personal preference.  This system makes it easy for students to return books to the appropriate bin and also helps to keep the bins organized.

If you'd prefer a more professional look consider using Avery stickers (available at any office supply store) instead of the small index cards. Avery stickers come on 8-1/2 x 11 sheets and can be run through your printer (which allows you to select your font). The stickers work just as well as the white index cards, but they are more costly.

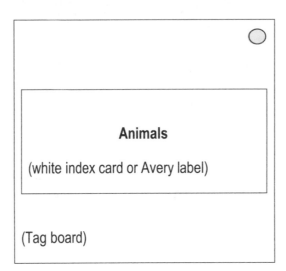

**Animals**

(white index card or Avery label)

(Tag board)

This system for labeling your collections makes the books even more accessible. Just think; you and your students can identify the category at a glance. And returning books will be quick and as simple as matching the color dots. So to label the remaining book bins in your classroom library follow the same procedure.

This system makes it easier for students to return books to the appropriate bin without supervision leading to greater independence. Any system or procedure used consistently over time will become a routine that develops confidence and competence across the year. Of course, like all procedures this must be practiced over and over again. You will need a monitor who checks bins at the end of each day to make sure all colored dots are in the correct tub.

You can search the web and find numerous examples of other ways to indicate the contents of each bin. Just go to your favorite search engine and type in labels for classroom libraries. The key is that you find one that works for you and stay with it for the school year.

## Keeping track of the books

If you purchase books with your personal funds we recommend that you write your name in permanent marker somewhere visible. This will make it easier to separate your personal books from those belonging to the school if you were to move to a new grade level or new school. Since we are in several schools each year and frequently use our own books in workshops we adhere address labels on the front cover of our personal books. You may find it useful to place a colored file label on the back of each of your personal books to make them easy to identify and sort if necessary.

## Making the Books Last

Since children will be handling the books and bins all year we recommend laminating the labels before attaching them on the bins so they will endure the use. When applying them to the end of the bins experiment with various tape and/or glue. We have found that wide packing tape works well, but your school librarian may have better suggestions.

When labeling the bins make it as easy and simple as possible for the children to identify, select, and return books. This system should be consistent across the entire year. While it is important for the space to be attractive and engaging you are intentionally designing an area that will serve as a powerful resource for you and your students in all areas of your curriculum across the day and throughout the year.

## Making them accessible

Once you have the bins labeled we recommend you place them on your shelves by frequency of use. Think about which bin of books will be most frequently used and place that in the priority spot and move on to the bin that will be used next most frequently and so on. It makes no sense to have the most frequently used bin in the most out of the way spot. The more frequently used bins would be on the most accessible shelf while the less frequently used bins would be place on the lower shelves. Once again, accessibility is the key factor here.

## On the Level

Organizing your library by leveling texts will make it both accessible and efficient. Your collection needs to include a broad range of titles and texts in both subject matter and reading levels to accommodate the typical spread of ability in your grade level. A collection of literature that has been leveled will be a valued resource when students are making selections for independent reading and working with the strategies you've modeled during reading instruction.

### Leveling makes the books accessible

You can purchase many books and collections of books that have already been leveled. This is helpful when establishing your classroom library. If you have books that you would like to level before adding them to your collection here are a few sources to assist you:

- www.librarything.com
- Scholastic Teacher Book Wizard
- **Leveled Books for Readers** by Gay Su Pinnell and Irene C. Fountas published by Heinemann.
- A software program called Intelliscanner with a free website at the initial cost of roughly $150.
- www.readwithmenow.com is an excellent resource (516-322-9575)

### Should the entire library be leveled?

There are differing opinions regarding the ratio of leveled books to books not leveled in classroom libraries. Some people recommend that 30% of the collection be leveled while others contend that any book not used as a read aloud should be leveled. We don't go to either extreme on this issue. We believe that a healthy portion of the library should be leveled so students can find engaging and interesting material for independent reading and research.

However, we do not believe that all books in the classroom library need to be leveled. We believe the leveled library should be generous and extremely varied in subject matter and genre. We believe that young readers need some time every day reading from the leveled books on their independent reading level to allow them to use the strategies they have been taught during guided reading and other instructional settings. If readers are attempting to read and develop strategies when the text is too difficult time is lost for them in developing proficiently. Center time or while one group is in guided reading is an ideal time for other students to be reading leveled books (and at any other time a reader chooses to go there).

At other times in the school day, readers should have the option to select books from other bins in the library regardless of level. We also strongly recommend that students be given a large block of time to lose themselves in books, to simply browse and explore. Think back to the analogy of the ice cream shop. The manager has a broad range of flavors on the menu so customers can explore and taste, try out new flavors and combinations, and bring in a friend to try a recent discovery. There are customers who return to the same flavor with the same toppings time after time. And other customers are more adventurous and desire to try something new. Your library needs to have a collection of tried and true comfortable material for readers. But it also needs to stretch them, to entice them to reach beyond. For example, you may have a text set of five titles on butterflies. That one set may contain two books that have been leveled to

give a less able reader access to the information. The remaining three titles are not leveled. The two leveled books in the set serve as a scaffold to build vocabulary and concepts that may spark interest and nudge the reader to explore the remaining three titles in the set. The remaining titles have rich illustrations, photographs, captions, headings, text boxes, diagrams, a glossary and an index. Perhaps the presentation as a whole is beyond the reach of this reader, but the two leveled books have given him basic vocabulary and concepts to whet his appetite for more information. Pouring over the remaining three books reading the captions with the various graphics, examining the illustrations/photographs and reading headings will generate questions. This book can become a focus of mutual interest between this student and a more facile reader where both will grow from the experience.

**Time with books, time for books, time for passion**

Remember the research on time spent reading and the need for both time and volume. Proficiency in reading takes lots of time and varied experiences to develop. Your classroom is the only environment where you have some control of how time is spent. Provide the time for reading so that students develop stamina and volume, develop confidence and competence, develop a love of reading and discover their passions and favorites. You can't assume this will extend into the home, so maximize the impact of the time you have using the resources at your disposal. Time with books is not always about "practicing" the skills and strategies. At times it is about pursuing a passion and every teacher has witnessed students engrossed in a book of intense interest like a hummingbird deep in a giant flower drinking the nectar. Those books are rarely on their current independent level.

The idea of devoting a block of time for falling into books is not a new one; teachers across the country have been doing this for years. You have most likely heard this idea referred to by many names including SSR (sustained silent reading), DEAR (drop everything and read), Independent Reading, Reading Recess (which Reba's school used), or Free Reading Block. It doesn't really matter what you call it. Give it any name that works for you and generates greater interest.

What matters is that you find a consistent time when students can practice strategies and engage in reading and have the opportunity to lose themselves in a book or other text. From our perspective this is not optional. Time for reading is essential to development of proficient and passionate readers. At this point in history we should understand clearly that proficiency without passion results in students who can but don't read. We need both.

Reader's Choice is another way to layer this practice into your schedule. During this time (20 to 30 minutes) students choose to buddy read or read alone. "Buddy reading" is when two students read together; more than two often turns into a social gathering. During reader's choice students may choose to read silently or read aloud. Special permission may be granted for a group to read together *if* they want to read a story in a Readers Theater format. During reader's choice students may choose to sit on the floor or move chairs to different parts of the room. But they are required to select one place to settle and stay there. You (the teacher) may be reading as well or you may choose to read with individuals or a small group.

### Self-selection and self-monitoring

When children are selecting books for the free reading block, take home reading, choosing books from the school or public library, or making selections in book stores if may be helpful for them to have some quick guide to finding a "good fit". The Five Finger Rule for selecting a book has been used by teachers and librarians for many years. Though clearly not infallible, it does offer a "quick and easy" means for self-selection. Remember, if the book is far beyond their reading level, the reader will become frustrated, comprehension will suffer, confidence will be eroded and valuable time will be lost.

**The five finger rule**

Choosing the 'just right book' is simple for a savvy reader:  Open the book and read a page.  For each word you don't know, hold up a finger. When you read to the end of the page count how many fingers you are holding up and use this guide:

- 1 Finger: Easy to read.
- 2 Fingers: Just right--enjoy!
- 3 Fingers: Challenging, but try it--you might like it.
- 4 Fingers: Very challenging--read with a partner.
- 5 Fingers: Too hard--save it for later, or have someone read it to you.

Show children how you select a book.  Tell them what other readers do when looking for something to read.  Here are a few things to remind them of:

- **The title**—does the title capture your attention?  Is this something you want to know more about?
- **The cover**—does the cover appeal to you?  What does it suggest? Does it evoke ideas in your mind?
- **Author**—is this an author I know?  Did I like other books by this author?  Is this an author I have heard other friends recommend?
- **Illustrations**—do the illustrations help me make sense of the book?  Do the illustrations capture my attention?
- **Genre**—is this a genre I have read before?  What do I know about this genre? What do I expect?
- **Blurbs**--read the summary and endorsements on the book cover and the inside flaps—do these give me an idea of what to expect in this book?  Is this topic or theme something that will interest me?

Too often children are intimidated by the number of pages, the size of font, the use of white space and the spacing between lines and this may lead to avoiding a book altogether.  Help children become aware of these as things to consider when shopping for books.

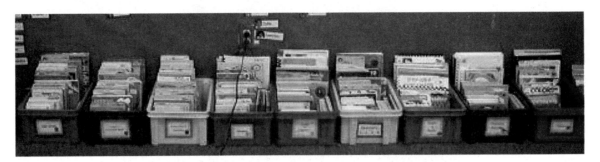

**Savoring a series**

When children find an author they enjoy, meet characters they love, or discover a series of interest, they may want to read more books by that author simply because the level and subject is comfortable. We believe they should be allowed to continue until they have satisfied the need or outgrown their interest in the characters, series, author or subject.

Many children will find comfort and success in a series and build confidence while resting on the plateau of the known. For example, we have known students who fell in love with Frog and Toad, Little House on the Prairie, Matt Christopher books, Junie B. Jones, Judy Moody, The Boxcar Children, or the Poppy series, just to name a few. There is a certain comfort that comes from knowing the characters and recognizing that the personality of each character remains stable across situations that vary. There is a certain predictable quality that makes a series an appealing option. As adult readers we do the same. When we visit the bookstore we generally look for a favorite author, a favorite genre, or the next book in a trilogy. Why should children be any different?

## Personalize collections for students

In many classrooms teachers develop book boxes with the children to use when time for 'free reading' occurs. This ensures that children are in their 'just right' books but also allows each child to make selections with the assistance of the teacher when needed. The boxes are developed on Monday, which saves time each day because children are not always shopping for new books. Remember, if the books are always too easy the reader will become bored very quickly and reading stamina will suffer while books that are too hard frustrate and repel children resulting in loss of reading growth. In Reba's former school, resourceful teachers used the large laundry detergent boxes with handles as book boxes to save money.

Need a reason to create the book boxes? Allington (2000) reminds us that sustained time with "just right" books

- is necessary for reading progress
- is essential to the development of fluency and comprehension
- is essential in for the development of reading stamina and engagement

## Management of the Library

Managing use of the library calls for the establishment of structures and routines. It will take several days or weeks for students to manage their responsibility for selecting and returning books, for the proper care of books, and for the organization of the library. These procedures have to be consistent and used on a daily basis, so be prepared to review them often.

The purpose of organizing (grouping books, labeling bins, applying the colored dots) is to create a structure to scaffold independence. You do not have time to go behind children keeping the area organized and neat. We recommend that during the first few weeks of school you demonstrate and practice procedures for selecting and returning books to the correct bin, where you store big books, how to place books in their home bins, and how to report if a book needs repair.

**Shopping for books: Learning to make wise selections**

Many children will spend too much time shopping for books so during the practicing weeks include a hint for a efficient selection to save time for reading. We know teachers who purchase inexpensive tote bags and invite students to shop on Monday for books to read during independent reading time across the remainder of the week. (See the book boxes mentioned above for a variation of this idea). Others allow children to exchange books daily. We encourage you to be aware of the habits students are developing and guard against the possibility of returning books so often that students don't spend time reading.

As you get to know your students you will see the patterns emerge in their book shopping habits. Reutzel and Fawson (2002) identify five types of shoppers:

1. **Binge Buyers** ---impulsively select books because of the displays.
2. **Discerning Customers** ---informed by others and generally select books that have been recommended.
3. **Social Shopper** ---turns the selection into a social occasion and wants to discuss each possible selection before making a decision.
4. **Convergent Customer** ---knows what they want when they enter the library area. These students make their selections quickly and return to reading as quickly as possible.
5. **Shop Till You Drop** ---take the entire time shopping with no time left reading. Keep your eye on this group and get them back to reading quickly.

We believe it is worth the time and effort to lead a few small group sessions on how to select books and to approach the classroom library with a plan in mind. You may find it beneficial to have a few former students come in for a visit and show your students how they made decisions from the library in your classroom. As each visitor leaves take a few moments to chart the suggestions. This chart makes an excellent reference when students seem to be aimlessly wandering in the classroom library.

If you use the book boxes or book bags to select a week of reading on Monday you need to decide whether they keep all the books until Friday or whether they return each book as it is finished. If your students are selecting books on an "as needed" basis, decide whether students will be allowed to return books as they finish reading and whether they are allowed to choose more at that time. The goal is to keep children invested in reading, so we feel students should be allowed to constantly return books and take new ones (unless this becomes an avoidance tactic and they are not really reading).

**Organization is crucial**

The time spent sorting books, labeling the bins and establishing procedures will pay off when students begin shopping for books. Remind students how books in the classroom library are organized (e.g. by author, curriculum content, theme, topic, genre) to make shopping easier.

Another helpful assistance to book shoppers is a "Recommended Reading Chart" posted in the library. Readers can use a Vis-à-vis pen to write their recommendations on a laminated chart. Each recommendation will include the title of the book, the name of students who might be interested and a comment about the book. Of course, post-it notes work just as well. Either format gives students a sense of responsibility and ownership of their reading.

## Checking out

Well if you are still reading and haven't run away screaming, then you are ready to create a procedure for the checkout and return of books in the classroom library. Our work takes us around the country and in oodles of classrooms each year. We are always on the lookout for a more effective and more efficient procedure. Here are a few suggestions we've gleaned for managing the circulation of books:

- Tape a library pocket in a back cover and insert an index card with the title written on the top. Make a poster with a library pocket for each student. As a book is selected, the student removes the card from the book, signs the card and places it in the pocket with his name on the chart. In a glance you can determine how many books any student has out, which books are out for the moment and where to look if a book is missing.
- Keep a loose-leaf notebook for students to sign when they remove a book. Turn to a new page with date stamped on the upper right corner each morning. When the book is returned the student draws a line through her name and stamps the current day next to the title.
- Print each student's name on a clothespin. When a book is selected the student clips the pin on the bin he took the book from. As the book is returned the pin is removed.
- Have students sign out only those books *they take home* using one of the methods above.
- Have a file box with cards for each student and ask the student to pull her name card from the file box and place it inside the bin where she selected a book. A variation of this is to have her write the book she is checking out on the card. She will need to check off or cross out when the book has been returned.

## Returning

The books are getting out there now and you have to decide how to get them back into the appropriate bin and accounted for. We have a few of suggestions for you.

- If the children are taught to look and match colored dots most can handle returning the book to the correct bin.
- Have a few children assigned to specific bins. For example, Erica is the monitor for the Folktales bin. All the books in that bin have an orange dot. Each day Erica does a quick audit of the books in the Folktale bin and pulls any book that isn't an orange dot. She brings the book to the monitor of the basket where the title belongs.
- Assign a monitor each week and have children return books to a large container such as a laundry basket reserved for returned books. The monitor would then return the books from the basket to the correct bins. This is an excellent opportunity for practice with sorting and categorizing. If this procedure is used work toward one of the other options listed above to increase individual responsibility.

As a teacher one of your primary goals is to lead children toward independence, so the procedures you choose to use in this area are an important component of your instruction. Begin the year practicing each of the procedures until your students understand the importance of the classroom library routines and take ownership of the space.

**Keeping track of books in the library**

After a few weeks of school you are likely to have one of those moments where you search the room looking for some book. You will swear you had a copy. Don't lose your sanity over this one; there are bigger issues to go nuts about. If you want an inventory of your library you may choose to invest in a database system. Amazon.com sells small scanners (for less than $100) that you attach to your computer. This little device will scan each of your books into the database. The initial procedure is quite time consuming, but it does provide a record of the number of books on your shelves and the genre of each. Though it may not be the most effective tool for checking books out with children, it will enable you to check inventory quickly and efficiently. Consider one for the school or grade level. Then you and your colleagues would know what resources lay within reach.

## Teaching children how to care for books

The classroom library is a significant investment of both resources and time. As such you need to teach students how to care for the books so they will be available throughout the year and for subsequent classes. If you see books crammed in desks or left lying on the floor, stop in that moment and make a big deal out of how sad it makes you and the author and the illustrator that books are treated so carelessly. Don't underestimate your power. Have you ever heard the statement, *where attention goes, energy flows?* Well it is true! You put your attention to the gentle care of books and your children will respond.

Each time you handle a book you are modeling the gentle care of books. Be conscious of your demonstrations. Think about it. Have you ever read aloud then pitched the book over on your desk? That action tells children it is OK to treat books in a cavalier manner. Do you dog-ear pages when reading a chapter book instead of using a bookmark? Think of what that suggests to students. Have you ever watched someone lick the tip of her index finger before turning a page? Have you thought of what that does to the page surface if this is done over and over----or just imagine the layer upon layer of germs if every reader picked up that habit from you----ugh! Become the model of the habits you wish them to exhibit when handling books. Think ahead to the consequences of children mistreating a book and/or the library. If it becomes necessary *close* the library for day. Remind them of their responsibilities. It may be necessary to have a list of procedures posted.

Establish a procedure for reporting any book that needs repair. For example, reserve a small bucket or basket as the *book hospital*. Have a clipboard where a note can be left stating what needs repair. We've read on the Internet about a special adhesive (*Aleene's Original Tacky Glue*) used to stick pages back in a damaged book. It is craft glue that is thick and flexible when it dries.

**Tips for making paperbacks last**

Collecting books can be an expensive venture, so a healthy portion of the library may well be paperback titles. We've seen several different methods used effectively for making much loved paperback books last several years. Here are a few of our favorites:

- Use the colorless, transparent book tape (like the tape used by librarians) on the spine of new paperback. You can also run a strip along the fold in the center page of the book before taping the spine. This tape is expensive but will make the book much stronger. Regular tape, like the tape used to seal boxes for mailing will work, but it is not as durable as the library tape.
- Colored duck-tape purchased at a building supply store like Lowe's will work but it obscures part of the cover of the book.
- All-weather Clear Poly-tape made by Manco can also be purchased at Lowe's and is cheaper than library tape and almost as good.
- Another option is to run the paperback cover through the laminator (if it is not too thick) and then trim so it will open. This works extremely well and keeps the cover nice and clean.

*A note of warning: Discuss with students what will happen if they cram paperbacks into book bags, desks, table cubbies or bins. Teach them that paper covers bend and tear unlike their hardback books. If a paper cover book should become damaged don't toss it out. Keep it as a reminder of the need to handle books with care.*

## Students Need the Opportunity to Read and Here Is the Proof

In earlier sections we made a case for increasing time spent reading and the positive impact that can have on overall literacy development.  We highlighted the need for building a rich, varied, and robust classroom collection and the importance of creating the space and routines to make it both attractive and useful.  Providing interesting books for children is a powerful incentive for reading, perhaps the most powerful incentive possible. This conclusion is consistent with research showing that extrinsic incentives (points, pizza, footballs...) for reading have not been successful, while improving access to books has been successful in encouraging reading. (Ramos & Krashen, 1998, p. 614).

The purpose of all this work is to lead students to toward independence in literacy.  That independence results in positive gains in reading achievement. Guthrie, Schafer, Von Secker, and Alban (2000) report that an abundance of trade books in the classroom predicted gains on statewide reading, writing, and science tests.  According to Krashen (2004), more books in the classroom leads to more voluntary reading, which, in turn, results in higher achievement. An increase in voluntary reading means students are more likely to read outside school.  Anderson, Wilson, and Fielding (1988) report that students who score well on standardized reading tests read far more outside of school than students who perform poorly on such tests.

## Reading Aloud to Children

Reading aloud to children should be a daily ritual, a routine event occurring several times each day. There are many reasons for reading aloud and there are several key times during the day when this can be done. However, for the purposes of this guide, one significant intention for reading aloud is to spark interest in the collection. Think of it as advertising. Read aloud to market the various topics, genres, authors and illustrators, themes and collections available in the classroom library. Read aloud to broaden your students' awareness of the possibilities, and offer suggestions after each reading for those who are interested. When you have read a book display it on an easel and surround it by other books that are similar in topic, by the same author, from the same genre, etc. Experience proves that books read aloud by the teacher are highly desirable for independent viewing and reading. [For more on Read Aloud see *Learning Under the Influence of Language and Literature,* Laminack and Wadsworth (2006); Reading Aloud Across the Curriculum, Laminack and Wadsworth (2006); *Unwrapping the Read Aloud* (2007) Laminack]

The classroom library is a resource. The full impact of its potential will never be realized unless students find their way in. Extend the invitation and enjoy the fruits of your efforts!

## Bibliography

Allington, R. (2000) *What Really Matters for Struggling Readers.* New York, NY: Longman.

Allington, R. (2009). *What Really Matters in Response to Intervention.* Boston, MA: Allyn & Bacon.

Anderson, R., Wilson, P., and Fielding, L. (1988). "Growth in reading and how children spend their time outside of school". *Reading Research Quarterly, 23,285-303.*

Calkins, L., (1986). *The Art of Teaching Writing.* Portsmouth, NH: Heinemann.

Cunningham, A., & Stanovich, K. (1998)."What reading does for the mind." *American Educator*; 22; 8-15.

Guthrie, J.T., Schafer, W.D., Von Seecker, C.,and Alban,T, (2000),"Contributions of integrated reading instruction in text resources to achievement and engagement in a state-wide school improvement Program" *Journal of Educational Research,* 93, 211-226.

Hiebert, E.H. & Reutzel,D. R (Eds.).(2010). *Revisiting Silent Reading: New Directions for Teachers and Researchers.* Newark. DE: International Reading Association.

Hill, B.C. & Ekey, C. (2010). *Enriching Classroom Environments.* Portsmouth, NH: Heinemann.

Krashen , S. (2004), *The Power of Reading: Inside From the Research.* Library Unlimited.

Laminack, L. L. (2007), *Unwrapping the Read Aloud.* New York, NY: Scholastic.

Laminack, L.L. & Wadsworth, R.M. (2006). *Learning Under the Influence of Language and Literature.* Portsmouth, NH: Heinemann Publishers.

Laminack, L.L. & Wadsworth, R.M. (2006). *Reading Aloud Across the Curriculum.* Portsmouth, NH: Heinemann Publishers.

Miller, D. (2008). *Teaching with Intention.* Portland, ME: Stenhouse.

Neuman, S. B. (1999). "Books make a difference: A study of access to literacy." *Reading Research Quarterly.*

Ramos, F. & Krashen, S. (1998), "The Impact of One Trip to the Public Library: Making Books Available May be the Best Incentive." *The Reading Teacher. 51(7):* 614-615.

Reutzel, D.R. & Fawson, P.C. (2002). *Your Classroom Library.* New York, NY: Scholastic.

Routman, R. (2003). *Reading Essentials.* Portsmouth, NH: Heinemann.

Taberski, S. (2000). *On Solid Ground.* Portsmouth, MA: Heinemann Publishers.

# About the Authors

Reba M Wadsworth is a former elementary classroom teacher and taught in three different states (Texas, Georgia and Alabama) from pre-K to sixth grade. She later worked both as an elementary guidance counselor and elementary principal. She now is a full time consultant and author. She has conducted workshops across the United States and presented at World Congress in New Zealand. She has written articles for various sources and is currently a contributing author-reviewer for the professional journal of the Alabama Reading Association and is a team writer for a federal grant to develop reading curriculum for the schools of Ethiopia. For more information about Reba, go to www.RebaWadsworth.com.

Lester L. Laminack is Professor Emeritus from department of Birth-Kindergarten, Elementary and Middle Grades Education at Western Carolina University in Cullowhee, NC. He is now a full time writer and consultant working with schools throughout the United States. He is author of numerous professional books for teachers and six pictures books for children with a new one upcoming this winter. He has served as co-editor of NCE journal *Primary Voices* and as editor of the Children's Book Review of the NCTE journal *Language Arts*. He served as a teaching editor and wrote the Parent Connection column (2000-2002) for *Teaching K-8*. For more information about Lester, go to www.LesterLaminack.com

He and Reba have co-authored two previous books: *Learning Under the Influence of Language and Literature (*Heinemann), *Reading Aloud Across the Curriculum* (Heinemann). They are collaborating once again on two forthcoming projects with Heinemann: *Bullying: Working Toward Kindness and Civility and Human Compassion. Taking a Proactive Stance Through Guided Read-Aloud and Conscious Conversation* and *The Writing Teacher's Troubleshooting Guide*.

# NOTES

# NOTES

# The Classroom Library Company Leveled Reading Chart

This leveling chart approximates how these leveling systems relate to grade levels and one another.

| Grade Level | Stages of Development | Guided Reading Level | Reading Recovery | Lexile | DRA | AR / ATOS |
|---|---|---|---|---|---|---|
| K | Emergent | A | 1 | Beginning Reader | 1 | 0.1 |
| K to 1 | Emergent | B | 2 | Beginning Reader | 2 | 0.9 |
| K to 1 | Early | C | 3 to 4 | 200 to 400 | 3 to 4 | 1.0 |
| 1 | Early | D | 5 to 6 | 200 to 400 | 6 | 1.1 |
| 1 | Early | E | 7 to 8 | 200 to 400 | 8 | 1.2 -1.3 |
| 1 | Early | F | 9 to 10 | 200 to 400 | 10 | 1.4 |
| 1 | Early | G | 11 to 12 | 200 to 400 | 12 | 1.5 - 1.6 |
| 1 to 2 | Transitional | H | 13 to 14 | 200 to 400 | 14 | 1.7 |
| 1 to 2 | Transitional | I | 15 to 16 | 200 to 400 | 16 | 1.8 - 1.9 |
| 2 | Transitional | J | 17 | 300 to 600 | 18 | 2.0 - 2.2 |
| 2 | Transitional | K | 18 | 300 to 600 | 20 | 2.3 - 2.5 |
| 2 to 3 | Transitional | L | 19 | 300 to 600 | 24 | 2.6 - 2.8 |
| 2 to 3 | Transitional | M | 20 | 300 to 600 | 28 | 2.9 |
| 3 | Self-Extending | N | | 500 to 800 | 30 | 3.0 - 3.9 |
| 3 to 4 | Self-Extending | O | | 500 to 800 | 34 | 3.0 - 3.9 |
| 3 to 4 | Self-Extending | P | | 500 to 800 | 38 | 3.0 - 3.9 |
| 4 | Self-Extending | Q | | 600 to 900 | 40 | 4.0 - 4.9 |
| 4 | Self-Extending | R | | 600 to 900 | 40 | 4.0 - 4.9 |
| 4 to 5 | Advanced | S | | 600 to 900 | 40 | 4.0 - 4.9 |
| 4 to 5 | Advanced | T | | 700 to 1000 | 50 | 4.0 - 4.9 |
| 5 | Advanced | U | | 700 to 1000 | 50 | 5.0 - 5.9 |
| 5 to 6 | Advanced | V | | 700 to 1000 | 50 | 5.0 - 5.9 |
| 5 to 6 | Advanced | W | | 800 to 1200 | 60 | 5.0 - 5.9 |
| 6 & Up | Advanced | X | | 800 to 1200 | 60 | 6.0 - 6.9 |
| 6 & Up | Advanced | Y | | 800 to 1200 | 70 | 6.0 - 6.9 |
| 7 & Up | Advanced | Z | | 800 to 1200 | 70 | 7.0 - 7.9 |
| 8 & Up, Mature Content | | Z+ | | | 80 | 8.0+ |

**Guided Reading Level**
The Fountas and Pinnell Leveled Book List, K-8 (2006 -2008 Edition), Fountas and Pinnell c2006, Heinemann

**Reading Recovery = Early Intervention Level**
"Reading Recovery" is a registered trademark held by the Marie Clay Trust in New Zealand, with Ohio State University in the US and the Institute of Education in the UK

**DRA = Developmental Reading Assessment Level**
Developmental Reading Assessment Resource Guide, Joetta Beaver c1997, Celebration Press

**Lexile = Lexile Level**
"Lexile" and "The Lexile Framework" are trademarks of Metametrics, Inc.